SMALL GODS OF SUMMER

To Sue —
Thanks for helping
my mother be
stronger.

Best,

Meg

SMALL GODS OF SUMMER

Poems by

Gregory LeStage

Antrim House

Simsbury, Connecticut

Library of Congress Control Number: 2013931011

ISBN: 978-1-936482-39-9

First edition: 2013

Printed & bound by Sheridan Books, Inc.

Book design by Rennie McQuilkin

Front cover design by Roddi Lignini

Front cover photo ("Nauset Sand") by William Lea Woodward

Author photograph by Mary R. Lamontagne

Antrim House
860.217.0023
AntrimHouse@comcast.net
www.AntrimHouseBooks.com
21 Goodrich Road, Simsbury, CT 06070

For Julia, my muse

ACKNOWLEDGEMENTS

Grateful acknowledgment to the editors of the following publications, in which these poems first appeared, some in slightly different forms:

The May Anthologies: "Your Bright Fiction"
Oxford Poetry: "Sunlight on Arles" (as "Sunlight on Provence"), "Your Bright Fiction"
Quadrant: "Evoking Voltaire" (as "The Principle of Predestination"), "Limestone Days," "To Make Time Slip" (as "Sending Cards")
The Reader: "A Dordogne Village Seen from a Bicycle," "As Intimacy Grew Perilous" (as "Men Grow Serious")

I would like to thank the following:

the Oxford University Poetry Society – advisors, members, events, history – for its formative role in shaping my commitment to the art;

the poet and professor, Jon Stallworthy, who taught me that one can be both a practitioner and student of traditional poetic form and delight in both;

Les Murray, Ian Hamilton and Seamus Heaney for expressing belief in me during my early years, a belief that fuels me still;

Bill Pierce of *AGNI* for his recent fuel of encouragement and guidance;

my mother, Linda, for her belief throughout; and my father, Donald, for passing on his love of words.

TABLE OF CONTENTS

III

IV

PREFACE

The poems in this collection represent years of work, not in terms of sustained effort but of time span between when it began and late 2012. A productive period in the early years, notable for its monastic focus, was interrupted by a hiatus of living – marriage, career, parenthood – that was followed by a more recent phase spent reexamining the past and staring down the present. This long interval afforded me the time to develop thematic lines that loosely define the book's four sections. It also gave me the freedom to experiment with form. Free and structured verse forms appear in each section.

The poems in Section I contemplate memory and its kin – nostalgia, regret, wistfulness. Those in Section II present various stages and angles of love, including beginnings and endings, wanings and creations. Poems about death past, present and future make up Section III. The main themes in the first three sections seem to coalesce in one character, the grandmothers that feature or cameo in a number of them. Section IV is a series of contemplations sparked by personal experience, philosophy, and insights gained through travel. There is some miscellany in here, too.

Memory is the strongest thematic vein in the collection. It is central in Section I and runs under the surface of many of the poems in the remainder of the book. There is the covert struggle to reconcile the truth of the present with the fiction of the past. There is the warping of perspective that results from only seeing the present through the past. Perhaps Miguel de Unamuno best explains my persistence with these themes in his observation that "the mind seeks what is dead, for what is living escapes it."

Above all, the collection represents a contemplation of the self and how it is formed by memory, love, and death while language strives mightily to report on all of it.

Be ahead of all parting, as though it already were
behind you, like the winter that has just gone by.
For among these winters there is one so endlessly winter
that only by wintering through it will your heart survive.

Rainer Maria Rilke
Sonnets to Orpheus (II, 13)

SMALL GODS OF SUMMER

Poems   Gregory LeStage

I

UNRING THE BELL

Make me one word that means
the nostalgia and sadness I feel
in the very moment
that is delighting me.

It must collect like a crucible,
that hollow bowl at the bottom
of a furnace that pools
what does not burn away.

It must fence-walk Janus-faced,
dervish on the pinhead of the instant,
see through a fish eye,
spell what Escher drew.

It must cyclone like regret,
all downdraft and disappearance,
and flywheel like hope,
that spindler of the bright side.

Then make me another word
that I can say in the aftermath.
A talisman that
unblinks the eye,
unsays the tell,
uncasts the die,
unrings the bell.

AT THE LAKE

for Matt

At the lake,
we are small and skinny and pink.
We ignore our mothers all afternoon
and secretly wait for our fathers to arrive.

Swimming is a struggle
not to touch bottom,
not to brush against the hairy underside of the dock,
not to drift over the shadow of the dock,
not to appear frightened.

We fish for perch with bacon
and a bamboo pole with a clackety reel.
It is a skill to avoid the hook, bravery to touch the fish,
which we only do because our sisters – girls –
won't even touch the graying meat.

The shallow pond in the back simmers
and smells worse than ever, we swear,
but leaves the tadpoles languid for the taking.
We catch them with scoops and put them in yellow buckets,
with silt and greasy green weed.
We have plans for them.

The diving board wobbles over a darkness
that we don't even dare each other into.
The diving tower, with the metal ladder sixty feet to the top,
then the pennant,

is simply inconceivable all day,
like a monument on a green,
until Uncle Jarvie arrives,
a dignitary endorsing a small event.

He waves before he climbs
in his penny loafers with the curled toes
and his trunks taut over his belly,
like the bathing cap over his head.
At the top, the earplugs insert and the loafers arch
in heel-over-toe tosses to the lawn.
Bits of tissue test the wind and drop without it.
Our eyes follow the upward swoop of arms
and the swanning arc,
as we forget the need to pee,
and he describes what will later be geometry,
intersecting the water.

We compete to count the ripples with our fingers
until he surfaces with his moustache,
then emerges, slickened, and strides away
to his scotch, waving,
as our lips blue and our fingers prune
and the gravel driveway crunches
with arriving fathers in ties and shined shoes.

AUGUST KETTLE

I pivot endlessly around
the scents of beachplum in breeze
and winding, hot jeep tracks that ease
past what the high tide sketched and left.

Heat simmers smells in August kettle
and evokes a day with whiffs of moments,
revolving on exaggeration – temporarily constant,
constantly momentary,

as constant and comforting as grandmother
perfumed, hovering, perspiring over me,
her hands, like fish, breaking the silent surface of my
afternoon, gliding over my messy hair
and reddening nose to dive back into
the glossy shallows of *Vanity Fair*.

This man-to-be with sand in his ears and grit in his jaws
is yet to leer at the beauty on the beach towel,
or to yearn for the familiar lines of that wrinkling face.
That bathing suit, heavy with sand and salt water,
is yet to reveal its meaning
in still, dried miniature on a peg,
holding the boy's shape.

Every step I took
among the steamy beds of seaweed,
the pungent, bleaching shells of shells,
and the jellyfish poaching in lavender pools
started up a little life

tenderly sorted, jarred, and labeled
in a pine-paneled bedroom,
seeping with pitch in that sultry month
when the air wishes it were water.

PENNIES ON THE RAIL

At dusk, I filled my pocket with pennies
and walked north out of my neighborhood,
slipping past cavernous Victorians haunted by low-renters
and over dirt lots where my grandmother
once flew her kite in the grass.

I skirted east along the main avenue,
where every third house slowly
sloughed its history onto the yard.
Men carpooled into driveways
past the litter of roof tiles and shingles.

I met a friend on the way,
and we snuck to the river bank
to single file down the tow path tightrope.
The water, palsied by the dam, smelled of metal.
The mill, just emptied of clockpunchers,
tilted at our backs.

At dusk, my father left his factory in his Chevy
and drove past the pasts he had inherited
as a son of the town,
his route home a downward spiral of byways
lined with flaking husks of foundries.
Nail salons and mini-marts obscured what was gone,
were palimpsests in neon.

At the footbridge, we felt late and ran
until we reached the chain link fence
that kept us from the rail bed,

the same fence that was not there
in my great uncle's stories of hobos
freely coming and going from tracks to river
to beg at the back doors of the grand houses
that lined the banks
and of how they were received by the rich.

We slunk like weasels under the fence
and up onto the blanket and ballast shoulder
to line our pennies on the rail,
split seconds, it seemed, before the 5:15 from Boston
rumbled past and flattened them into ovals and oblongs,
good luck pieces.
In our palms, they burned and cooled and shined
with only the faintest trace of their original design.

Back at home, my father,
newly arrived with his own flattened sense,
fingered my treasure
and told me that when he was my age
he gave all of his copper
to the war effort.

SEEKING AND FINDING

On a winter walk in middle age
around the periphery of a field,
where the grass meets the thicket then the woods,
I lapse into the age-old boys' rite
of searching for baseballs – head down,
feet clearing leaves, eyes on the soil.

Back then, a hit deep into the brambles
was a homerun and, often, the end
of the game, which then started another
of seeking and finding under the pines.
Our Indians hid in the undergrowth.
Our Cowboys died in the open.

We once surprised a whole tribe hiding
in a great heap under a cedar grove.
A Harvard archaeologist arrived
and inserted his trowel in the earth
like a cake knife and served us a slice
of a Nauset shellfish midden.

From this centuries-old dump –
this deep and narrow archive of one thing –
he dug surgically and narrated richly,
while we crouched, watched and listened
as a civilization flowered
around those natives shucking clams in the shade.

I am left to recover myself
in a buried, decomposing baseball,

that perfect little skull of a man's game
with a boy's rules; in a perfect sapling
that might have been a bow; in a
backwoods bed of pine needles
on which to lie in wait or perhaps to rest.

THE MAILMEN

We called ourselves The Mailmen in a chant
as we loaded the back seat with our deliveries,
Louisville Sluggers past their ball yard use.

In a borrowed wreck of a sedan
we rolled through some tony suburb
with the headlights off and the radio on.

We smoked cherry tobacco
from my father's briarwood pipes
and traded lies in the haze to jack ourselves up.

One of us wore a black concert t-shirt.
Others had black velvet posters on the insides
of our closet doors that we would not admit.

The driver threatened to take us to see
this slut he knew and held up a certain finger
to signal his intentions, while our lust danced with our dread.

Then the slow approach to the mailbox
and the body half out the window to deliver
the buckling blow by baseball bat.

The victim vomited its paper innards
onto the street; its jaw swung slack on the hinge.
The peel-out was our squealed climax.

We bayed at the passing streetlights
and took the vandal's oath,
with fingers crossed behind our backs.

SMALL GODS OF SUMMER

We were minor deities in a small seaside town
that had no major ones.

You may not have not heard of Aeolus,
who made the West Wind gentle,
or of Palaemon,
who guarded the harbors,
or of Glaucus,
who grew fins and a tail and rescued fishermen.
But let me assure you:
They were heralded by their locals
and known to each other.

The sun shone narrowly on our square mile
and brightly on us, bleached and bronzed us,
left us vaunted, hollowed us out.
We filled ourselves up with the fleeting
and fantastic.

We loitered and appareled ourselves
by the never-wine-dark sea.
We overspent on sunglasses and beach britches
to cut the right figure on boats and boards,
to photograph valorously on waterskis.

To avoid rigors of the mind,
we watched drive-in movies
from lawn chairs on truck beds.
We cut each other's hair and grilled meat
to honor the triumphs of the day.

At beach parties,
bonfires flattered our burnished faces.
We danced to funk unconvincingly,
but with verve.
Beer made everything possible.

The girls were forgiving;
so were the police, mostly.
We were never in the newspaper
for doing good or evil, because we did neither.

We worked outdoors with our hands and in crews
to lighten the load, to fill the holes and silences.
We calloused as the dull work dulled us down,
but the milling and mining for laughs was sweet toil.

Soft-served glances and phone numbers
passed over snack shack counters
were shiny, witty lures
often cast, seldom taken.

We shared odes to the ones that got away
and made up tales about the ones we caught.
Talk built the temple of our brotherhood,
was the confection of our immortality.

Tragically, we did not die.
We mellowed, thickened, thinned.
We preserved our mythology,
like curators of one of those tiny village museums
that no one else visits.

THE TRACTOR

The gleaming red tractor coughs
its way around the field
making crop circles,
a beacon in the grain at high noon.

My young daughter is wicked
at the wheel, and the waist-high
wheat lies down in the chance
shapes of her whim.

Downwind, I smell its purpose.
From a distance, I feel its 4-cylinder
percussion in my chest
and its 2,400-pound tread in my soles.

Its displayed engine and cast iron spine
are a spectacle of torque.
The sound of its muffler
is the growled answer to the equation of its parts.

Its ethos is pure 1940, is harrowing.
A fleet of 12,000 row-cropping
the country out of the Depression
and into the war.

My girl knows none of this,
only its red beauty, simple power,
and my wordless bond with it,
my sepia-tinted fixation.

She sketches and photographs it,
remarks how prettily it pairs with our 1840s farmhouse.
She bestows an Old Testament name upon it
and concocts a matching personality.

When I park it under her treehouse
it is a tractor on an old farm,
and she is the struggling farmer
or his hardbitten wife.

When I hook it up to a creaky hay wagon,
it delivers a load of children
to the water's edge
and idles in the shade while they swim.

At twilight, it cools and drools oil
in the wings of the wagon,
which is now a stage for girls dancing
to an audience of waving wheat and clapping parents.

At midnight, it silhouettes something hunched and ready,
something male and equine.

A CIA OPERATIVE WRITES TO HIS SON

My Dear Boy,

The weather in Vienna is noteworthy
for its low cloud cover and humidity.
I recently remarked on the way the mid-
afternoon sun lay on the Karlsplatz facades
and revealed what the architects must have meant.
I spoke of it at length with a confidante.

The Berlin Wall provides opportunities,
depending on one's perspective.
Grafitti on the west and blank on the east.
The division is so literal, so clear.
From the cleaving flows
the job-securing spawn of secrets.

Speaking of walls,
have you used the Berlin Defense I taught you
when your opening moves were weak?
1 e4 e5 2 Nf3 Nc6 3 Bb5 Nf6
has long had a reputation
for solidity and drawishness.

Did you read the *Times* piece on Archibald MacLeish?
Such discretion, such direction of facts and figures!
And we know none of it.
We envy him his gridiron moves and poems
because they are feints.
Think of his talents arrayed across his selves!

I encourage you to write.
Meter and rhyme tap out in cadence and sound
everything they need to know and no more.
They reveal just enough of all that you conceal.
The exquisite code hides you in plain sight –
the steak the burglar throws the dog.

If you're following the news,
you'll infer that my Prague spring
forsook summer and fall and turned to winter,
like what you'd expect from Moscow.
It holds me in that gelid place
between thought and action, from which I write.

Looking backward and forward
is holding mirrors up to mirrors.
An infinity of reflections,
but not one with me in it.
Promotions are my reward for this.
In my advance, though, is my retreat.

THAT ISLAND, MEMORY

When I walked into the street lamp's glow,
the hooligans surged like fire ants
carrying out their imperative.
With shaven heads and unshaven mandibles,
booted and fisted
they stung me with broken beer bottles
then frenzied into the darkness,
alight with angel dust and lager,
as I sprawled inert with their toxins
coursing and spiraling me into amnesia.

In the fluorescence of the emergency room,
the doctors described the rupture and removal
of the before self,
who once strode under the street lamp,
from the after self,
who lay stitched, swollen and oblivious.

My brain, bent on self-preservation,
had formed a junta of chemicals that abducted
those thirty seconds under the street lamp
and exiled them to an unmappable, unreachable island
to keep them from conspiring into a memory
that could disrupt my fragile inner peace.
And then the deft and instantaneous
blotting of the microfilm
and expunging of the records
for the good of the state.

And, years later, this vain preoccupation
with those islanded selves
that will never accrete to my frayed whole,
that lie just beyond the glow of all those street lamps.
And now the insistent question,
Who is the I that knows the bodily me?

II

LIMESTONE DAYS

We had already metamorphosed our soft limestone days into marble
when we came upon ourselves in a quarry eagerly cutting
them into blocks for others to chisel and polish
and remembered that we had expected to be working
and blending the three-shaded clays
of morning, afternoon, and evening
into numberless rows
of terra cotta urns awaiting
our content.

SOMEONE FLOATS IN YOU

16 January 1998

On Sunday, September 14
when I was in medieval Rye,
anonymous in Little Orchard House,
thronged by histories, wattled and daubed by what was,
         and feeling pastless,
you phoned from London to oracle something
    so brand new,
    so hidden,
    so true.

For five years
we have been growing in us
without proof.
But now someone floats in you
and gives evidence,
and makes promises for our past.

BEESWAXING THE CRIB

I will beeswax the spindle crib
in sections
and have a tiny new boxspring made
and a tiny new mattress.
I will use a soft cloth
and spread the wax evenly.

I will think of my grandmother, aged 17 in 1922,
unclouded by having no child, no beau,
staring in the window
of a Martha's Vineyard antique shop,
looking at this crib,
thinking of my mother thinking of me thinking of you.

When I'm done,
I will put the perfect fitted sheet on
and, bending over,
will think of you there,
curled like a comma, or a question mark.
I will look at you and make reconsiderations.

I will leave one small section unwaxed
so that I can do this again even after you are born,
this looking forward.

Dairy Barn Wedding

For Adrian and Alice

What it is now is not what it was.
Husbandry was manifest.
Production cycles whirred:

Silage to udder, udder to milk,
milk to market, market to table.
Machines marshalled everything.
The weather was bovine, was lactose and oil.

Then someone made a decision;
time and quiet moved in.
The only whirr was swallows.
The whiff went to wood.

Inside went whitewash bare.
The floor went to smooth slab,
and the space opened wide
to the new sacraments.

In go the long tables and cloths.
Up go the white string lights.
Chairs and flowers are arranged.
The sun sets in high ribbons.

People arrive with their hearts
and shape them into words

that children act out in those
joyous movements they make at gatherings.

Music joins and binds,
as do steak and drink and cake.
Toasts turn into crystal.
Fireworks peony in the windowpanes.

The vast cathedral ceiling
– heavily beamed yet spreading
its load to weightlessness –
now arcs a meaning beyond its purpose.

APOGEE TO PERIGEE

For Thaddeus and Carrie

You two: here is an ancient lovers' rite – lie
on a rooftop, in a meadow or on the beach,
with the earth relinquished below you. Each
trace your love in the night sky.
With your fingers, race to the polestar.
Plunge into a nova or quasar.
Catch and release a comet.
Look into each other, and name it.

Hand in hand,
calculate the odds of your union.
Rejoice in the sheerness of its unlikelihood
by dancing dances dancers dance,
reeling in perfect ovals, like moon and planet,
in retreat and advance
from apogee to perigee.
Go to the bedroom.

In the morning,
descend the stairs.
Pass the mail on the floor.
Ignore the dishes in the sink.
Avoid the headline's warning
and your faces in the mirror there.
Do not think; try not to blink.
Open a door.

Enter a room.
Run your palm across a dusty surface.
Look at it together.
See the final incarnation of ghosted meteors,
powdered asteroids,
the spin-off of nebulae,
the atomized splendor of planet creation.
Embrace.

Then behold the dust floating
in a cylinder of sunlight:
celestial bodies in diorama,
spiraling in a system.
Watch it settle,
making neither sound nor difference.
Boil the kettle.
Kiss.

AS INTIMACY BECAME PERILOUS

As intimacy became perilous, its risks foretold,
my father was prepared and renounced it
methodically,
like sweets or gin or verse,
and secured passage.

Assenting women, drawn in,
basked in broken relief
about the jagged rocks,
or strolled near boneheaps,
near shells of men,
and thrived on urgent whispers.

He barked commands to peers:
Lash me to the mast!
Ignore my naked pleas!
Forget my secrets, my caprices.
They stoppered their ears
and hastened to the task
at desks, golf courses, and bars,
pulled hard on mid-life oars,
saving themselves with wordless pacts
in a conspiracy of beeswax,
as he listened, flirted, implored
and, as arranged, was safely ignored.

AN ACTUAL LOVE

Now you excuse each other the silly things,
the mild irritants of oversight and innocence,
like the tap curiously left running again,
or the lids left off jars
and conversations.

Later, you will probably tolerate
those precious childhood stories
and their minted replicas.
One of you might accept the iron will be left out,
while the other might tolerate the iron will.

Even still, it is all so new.
The trickling recurrences cut no channel
in your expectations.
There is no deluge, no galaxy.
Only the dribble and orbit of the small.

In time, you could even be convinced
that you will excuse each other
the lipstick trailing upward in the cracks,
the clockwork clearing of phlegm,
the processed hairdo, or the thinning of it,

the way of wearing those trousers,
the days canyoned by routine,
the ice trays in frozen overflow,
the 5 o'clock pouring of the drinks:
yours like this, mine like that.

By then,
you will be inseparable in silence,
distant in sheer proximity,
as in bed,
as in two planets.

But what is not possible to know
is that one of you
will never pardon the other
for the supreme betrayal of going first,
for being left

to peel back the loss
to expose the lacuna
and admit that the mourning
is not just for what is no longer,
but for what never was.

SONGS ABOUT LETTERS

There will be no more songs about letters
written with tears or blood on them –
the licked stamp and the wait,
the postman as Hermes,
the unrewarded rush to the mail box –
because heartbreak and longing,
avowal and plea
will not find voice on stationary.

There will be no more songs about calls
made with dimes and intervening operators
from booths where rings rang without end,
or where breakups were sealed in
and steamed up the glass,
as the phone book swung slack on a wire,
a dead bird hung by its leg,
because we won't need the closed space or coins.

We will type everything in the open,
in the here and now.
We will not suffer delay
or agonize over which word to ink
or regret what was inked
because we will trade briskly in the instant recant,
blithely in amends.
This rapid cycling of thrills will be our coca leaves.

All calls will be answered, all messages delivered.
There will be no time or quarter for
the sentinel of anticipation,
no pausing to pine in the eddies of the hour.
Feeling the pinch and pang of drawn-out silence
will be like reading about perfume.
Too many songs will be about the buzz
of moments, their meanings like mayflies.

III

A PERFECT SHAPE

Some French thinker wrote that
the egg and the Coca-Cola bottle
are the most perfect designs
because they combine the strong and the brittle
in individual lines that have a certain inevitability,
a collective, almost molecular, intent
to describe completeness.

I saw such a design in my child
when she formed the shape of compassion
for a schoolmate with a terminal illness
when both were too young to grasp it.
She sensed only the grasping,
the abstracted, slow motion freefall,
and drew the lines to contain it.

She helped him form words
with his lips and pencil
when he fell behind forever.
She stood next to him in chorus
to thicken his tinning voice.
She let him win races sometimes,
praised paintings that looked like accidents.

She told him he was normal
and held him to account
when he broke schoolyard codes,
just like everybody else.
You're only as special as I am,

so just be like me
was the unwhispered password.

And she never told us.
We heard it from the sick boy,
who manifested the design
and completed the shape with his telling.
Strong and brittle inverted.
She collapsed into tears
under the dead weight of his happy account.

FORCE MAJEURE

d. February 14, 2010

The day my father's heart shook and stopped,
aftershocks in Haiti convulsed towards Chile and Turkey
down arteries of fire.
Collapse was categorical.

Help descended on the rubble of his house,
where order was forced to yield.
Dust plumed around his possessions and would not settle,
as the telephone formed a bucket line of words.

The ambulance delivered his body to the hospital,
and the search began.
Rescuers at the scene vied with looting
enzymes that overran cells, shattered molecules, stole time,
while salvagers probed chambers and walls
seeking the crushed and misshapen;
looked through apertures and into cavities for a future;
saw promise in two clear, domed regions where light once entered;
plumbed the superior vena cava for signs;
secured a furrowed plain eligible for swift harvest.

Pure caritas were his alms of skin, bone, and sinew.
There was rapture in two supreme cornea
and clemency when the epicenter heart, beyond redemption,
was jarred and shelved as a curiosity.
Then he and the grateful burned, the beseeching blind
became each other, hence whole –

he, in a state of grace; they, in repair.

We razed the remains and filled in the fault lines.
We will archetype new structures and symmetries
and rebuild on old ground.
All of the materials will be new.
We will furnish with fable and gild with figments.
Gloss will give everything a reflective quality.

NEW WIDOW

Searching and yearning are the centrifuge
whose sediments pollute her calendar,
checkbook, thermostat, closets, and pantry
and settle into her childrens' faces
when they step through the door on holidays.
What she divines is behind her returns
for tea, fades, reappears at dawn, wanes, waits.

Grief seizes the pencil, drafts the checklist,
then sidetracks her with other suggestions.
It sows clutter as she tidies the house.
It confesses to his silent ashes
while she eavesdrops at the door and takes notes.
Isolation is the mute intimate
that indulges all of her dark questions.

But what if she buoyed in grief's trough, rose
with its swell, surged ahead of its crest, rode
its forward falling spiral, broke with it,
and propagated its disturbances,
then repeated the above in somber
elation, in joyless affirmation?
Wouldn't she manifest a primal truth

and go forth whole when the wave motion stopped?
She could caw her lament with the ravens
at a funeral for one of their own,
and wring and rue at an elephant's wake
in its pageant of swaying and touching.
She could know their flight, their lumbering on –
that every cell thrums with consummation.

HER KITCHEN WAR ROOM

In her kitchen, there is no they.
There is a she – a breakfast table dispatch center
receiving condolences and sending thank you notes
as if through pneumatic tubes.
Mourners slip under surveillance and con security
to pass casseroles through the screen door.
The phone is a two-way tunnel between dark and light.
She's pushpinning territory where she's newly been.
Fresh facts and floral arrangements await placement.

DEATH OF A EULOGIST

The first one took the heaviest toll,
even though its gem-cut words seemed to roll
from his lips semi-preciously
and drew baubles of tears expectedly
from the mourners who came to validate the deceased,
who came to collect the amulets,
who came to catch the words he released
into the air above them like gauntlets
for living a worthier life.

He was exhausted and out of breath:
the end of the service was a death.
But he was resurrected by praises
and claims of how certain phrases
simply reflected everything –
hieroglyphs deciphered to reveal a civilization.
These voices hymned his calling
and chorused into the revelation
that he could spin gold from the grasped straws of the bereaved.

The third and fourth deliveries in his small town
made the newspaper. The words he had sown
were Delphic: he was a grace-bringing curtain-dropper
who made silver from the copper
of average lives in need of affirmation
of what they did and did not do.

Some said that he brought more comfort than the ministrations
of the ministers by bejeweling what was true
with what glittered.

He had lost count by the time he was called
to serve a person of great eminence. He was enthralled
by the crush of witnesses in a vast open field
who came to receive his yield,
which formed the basis for a novel and then a screenplay.
He retained the rights – it was *his* story –
but received no pay,
knew no further glory,
because he died abruptly and young.

He had written his own eulogy
and left strict instructions to ensure that its delivery
opened the ark of his covenant
and scorched what came before it.
His words divined the arc of the unlived
behind the profoundly worked.
They illuminated what a craftsman contrived –
a life that forked
and took the road others traveled.

His words exposed a man afraid
to be vagabond, to ease from shadow to shade,
to scatter petals in the current
and just follow where they went,
to let them sink or sluice out of sight,
to flow on through days that are inexplicable
and through nights that are bright
with the unknowable
and, as such, are transcendent.

AN OXFORD PROFESSOR'S BEQUEST

Lecture-room logic and well-taken sherry
decorate the tenure of the cloistered mind.
A life somewhat in print, somehow too wary
of the dilemma – to be clever or kind? –
stands in unfrequented cabinet: dusty books,
protected behind steel cage, display in jest
the sum total of Professor Gibson's Bequest.

He died just recently enough
to have a good showing of paperbacks
displayed just decently enough
in accidental piles and happenstance stacks,
or lying like wastrels against pillared hardcovers:
jaundiced, musty, artificially unaged,
exhibiting the thinking he waged.

The commemorative plaque
is an index card inscribed in lead
and riveted with a rusty tack,
honouring what he often said:
I shall be quoted.
Spines soaked in pipe smoke
support words others spoke.

In a dozen forgetful fellows
stand a dozen oak-paneled figments
where his unpainted portrait sallows
and renders his most telling moments:
asleep in the library, mouth agape, head tilted,
miming query to higher things
and what that supposedly brings.

TO MAKE TIME SLIP

I am sending
more and more and more
postcards to my grandmother now.
It is like flipping playing cards into a hat,
or any of those things you do
to make time slip quietly away,
or stop slipping.

She and I are both changing.
On seeing me, she says,

You look more and more like your grandfather.

I approach her like something filigreed,
but in my hug she becomes
a warm, cardiganed
bag full of hangers.

You even hold me the way he used to.

KNOWING

My knowing grandmother
leaves her purple fuchsia hanging
to die in September
she is so sure of life in spring.

EVOKING VOLTAIRE

My grandmother unwittingly evokes Voltaire
when she tells me
that everything works out for the best
in this world.

I only picture that Frenchman,
after the glove across the face
and the choice of weapons,
armed with the final word
to slash predestination
as an explanatory principle.

My tongue has no parry to
There's no going back to the past.
What's gone is gone.
It was meant to be, dear.

Your Bright Fiction

If I have a choice, you will wean me away from you
carefully and tenderly, without drawing too
much attention to the details of the weaning,
and turn a weekend's or a month's visit away
into a fully-expected, full-season stay,
then into an entirely predicted move – this meaning

that you will then transform slowly into an old friend
whose lengthy letters and regular postcards tend
to grow shorter, less personal, and less frequent
over time, until recorded correspondence
is replaced by love alone and the planned-for sense
that the foreseen separation is permanent.

To ease me on, I will not want to hear you talk
anymore. I will just want to listen – as I walk
down your path, through your house, by your flower beds –
to people talk about you. Over time, through
recalling such talk, your bright fiction will fade to true.
I will smile as portraits unyellow and the present weds

the past in a ceremony when I present
you with these words. Then we will vow that they are meant
to stay sealed and be opened at another, more
forgetful time. You will understand, with a light heart,
as the choir and bells subside and the engines start,
that I will not see you to the door.

IV

MY COYOTE

Watching me from the woods' edge is my coyote,
the same one that would lie in wait under my boyhood bed.
He is no vision, though, no fleeting creation of peyote.
He lives on because he has been fed.

We learned to keep our distance over the years.
He stayed clear of the house, I of the wood.
But the musk of my thoughts and fears
kept him in the neighborhood.

And now he has a litter of pups.
There is no mystery about their conception.
At night, they slice through the walls in yips.
His howling is my reception.

UMBRELLA FORGETTERS

We cannot tell the umbrella forgetters
from the mattress tag removers,
the pen losers
from the late night red light runners.

And neither the church skippers
from the strip club gropers,
the under-the-tablers
from the dine-and-dashers.

The grifter and shell gamer look alike.
So, too, the counterfeiter
and the cop in plainclothes.
There is bliss in this blindness,

but then a sudden burst of light
reveals that certain thread-thin lines
– the clerical collar, the whistle around the neck –
barely divide the trusted and the wicked:

it is the camera flash
on the courthouse steps
that captures the other face of
the priest and boys club director;

the hologram that slightly pivots
to present the skull
with its funhouse rictus,
bony hand and candy rosary;

the spear of sun that strikes the scales
of the hooked fish on the boat
and reveals the wretchedness
under the iridescence;

the flashlight beam in the mirror
that briefly bewilders,
the slow dawning of implication,
of aiding and abetting.

INHERITANCE

Our ancestors display their possessions
in our houses and guilt us
into a one-way dialogue about origins.
They insist on reverence when we wind their clocks,
instruct on our arrangement of their furniture,
preach that the straight legs
of the Federal style were preferred
over the immodesty and excess of curves and gilt.

They position their Revere bowls
to pool the sunlight and their portraits to shun it,
because one receives and holds and the other fades.
Their silverware, passed down like a writ,
voices the short, sharp language of the monogram
from inside velvet-lined chests.
We hear it and obey by setting the table
in the customary way.

And this discourse with our forefathers
is blazoned in brass block letters
on our colonial village greens:
He who has no feelings of veneration for his predecessors
should expect none from those who follow him.
Their rectitude and heirlooms are portable,
so we take them with us when we colonize
conversations and houses in unfamiliar territory.

ROOTS

The Seri tribe of Sonora have been told
the ancient things about earth's possessions,
of which they are one.
They are rooted, roots hold them;
they are roots themselves.
They have more than fifty words
for blood relationships
and countless more for land.

Their roots speak when they ask,
Miixoni quih zo hanta no tiij?
Where is your placenta buried?
The elders know the exact spot
where their afterbirth
was placed in the ground,
covered in sand and ash
and topped with rocks.

They know that everyone has a flower inside,
and that inside the flower is a word.
But they are disappearing
and with them the tongue they use
to water the soil and the flower,
to feed the roots
they tend on behalf of those
who came before and who will come.

IF SEVEN THANES

If seven thanes are going to haul out
the priceless hoard from the slain dragon's lair
while others fetch logs from the wide woods
to stack and deck your towering pyre;

If they are to kindle your funeral fire,
weep in the woodsmoke,
and rue in the rage of the flames
as your bone house burns brightly;

If a woman, standing apart, is to wail
above the cries with her palms upward
and spew cataclysms of dread
undammed by your death;

If your people are to have scouted
a headland for your mound
and will have made sure to build it broad
so that the gods will notice it;

If the leavings in your cindered pile
are to be worthy of your barrow
and are to hold their value beyond the vale
when they are later looted;

If twelve warriors are to gallop
around your tomb chanting dirges
of all that you did,
what kind of man must you have been?

Will you have provided and protected,
taken the right risks, given gifts
with the grace and greatness of a fair mind?
Or will you have sat by and made hope your strategy?

SUNDAY AFTERNOON

after Wallace Stevens

> "We feel the long pulsation, ebb and flow of
>   endless motion,
> The tones of unseen mystery, the vague and
>   vast suggestions of the briny world, the
>   liquid-flowing syllables..."
>   – Walt Whitman, "In Cabin'd Ships at Sea"

i.

Roused by rum, the journalist relaxes
into her foreign sun and cheery sarong.
A wave dismisses the cabana boy
and the served coffee and oranges.
Pungent sweat and citrus are not for her.
She sets her gaze, listens to her mind, and
contemplates the parakeets that fly low
across her field of vision and beyond:
she's sure no view is wider than the eye,
freedom is no greater than its holder,
freedom is the mastery of the known.
This issue is settled for the thousandth
time, even as it pecks, squawks and takes wing
with the question that pours the rum without
the tonic of an answer, a story
that will sustain her under wide water.

ii.

She wades in the tepid sea and wonders:
Do I risk floating and treading? Do I plunge?
Her assurance is a stagnant lagoon,

she decides, and breaks the surface forever.
Once over her head, certainties take on
water, reshape in new salinity,
slithering away and weaving through holes
in the submerged reef of her lexicon,
hanging diaphanous, like seahorses
curling in query, in permanent pause.
She sees shadows that dart, glance by and wind
around and elude their solid contour.
She surfaces between implications,
orients herself to the dominion
of the cabana and emerges dry.

iii.

Freed of her artifice, utterance comes
when she wakes during the night without thought
and looks down at it all and sees that black,
bottomless color, curved over distance,
that is midnight over open water –
and fearing its quintessential embrace,
and seeking suspension in that embrace,
and desiring powerlessness in it,
and accepting the sad, striving plight
of language, of shaped sound as a means of
revealing her divinity to her.
Her mute, satisfied surrender to depth
proves freedom is fate, silent discourse is
nature, imagination our making
and our self-sanctified undoing.

A Dordogne Village
Seen from a Bicycle

When you get closer,
as the road begins to imply its intent,
you begin to hear the permanent
and the temporal
argue it out in a village:
halcyon or obsolete, pastoral
or indifferent.

Small brick barns, lofts, and houses,
smaller wooden hutches, coops, and sheds
kept upright by the green resolve
of ascending and descending vegetation,
and the grass, now wild and pristine,
turned to grasses
and reaching up in individual blades,
and ubiquitous moss
layering like shingles,
and apricot tiles
cascading like ivy down swaybacked roofs,
and the fork in the road,
rationing only one choice –
all dispute with industry's synthetic advance.

You have time to wonder about
progress, then decline and, finally,
some new beauty,
as stone walls lead you out
and diverge and spill like conversations

between the lifetime farmer and his city sons,
unmended in places.

Then the lane urges you towards old men
who were expecting you
and who offer chèvre from the walnut-shaded verge,
or green bottled beer without labels from their café,
which is also the post office
although there is no sign.

A hamlet We Had Come Not to Expect

Heard from the road,
a distant bell chimed the illusion
of a hamlet we had come not to expect
until we rode

into the dispersing conclusion
of a christening, as the bell reprised respect,
and, despite our entrance,
we still felt the distance,

like pagans arrived on machines,
as the inviolable congregation
looked at us, and we looked at them
across the square's cobblestone chasm.

SUNLIGHT ON ARLES

Only Van Gogh evaded that clear,
unambiguous candor of atmosphere,
in which everything has its due place and proportion
and stands exactly where it is.

Through a clinic window,
his self spread outward to stir the light,
and the two vibrated in unison,
in whorls and curls of color,
through shadows troubling in wreaths,
through skies schooling in blueness,
like fish,
like a surface broken from a thrown stone,
like a wrong word in his ear.

He looked into the indiscriminate light,
and built frames around the open space.
He reduced it to permanence,
returned it to its connotations.

THE PAINTED CAVES

Michelin and *National Geographic*
kept the painted caves at a distance,
colored, selective, and epitaphic
to our minds only, faint remembrance.

But when our eyes adjusted in the damp
of those dark galleries underground,
perspective flickered from a tallow lamp,
and there we felt connected and found,

unexpectedly, maybe for the first time,
in a sketched and tinted room,
where matter suffused with the sublime
then calcified in a carved continuum

of animals and signs migrating through
the millennia losing meaning,
retaining Beauty, preserving the hue
of a truth far too deep for gleaning.

What great impulse summoned their skill,
their visions, longings, fears and beliefs,
pushed them into the darkness to fulfill
this urge to create eternal motifs?

DRIFTING THE BAY

Past the summer's end, I drift the bay
away from the changing waters and the day
that plunge and cool below in the season's flow.
The imperative is chronic, true and slow.
Delicate aster blossoms and salt marsh hay
bend in the ebb, and tentacled flowers sway
to paralyze their drifting and pendent prey.
Quahogs bed, eels ribbon towards the Sargasso
past the summer's end.
Scallops propulsing up the river array
acres of intent. I just float to display
my assent, while the jellyfish flamenco
and fencing blue crabs feint, jab, and know to go.
Distant fathoms pull, but I resign to stay
past the summer's end.

About the Author

Gregory LeStage lives in Cambridge, Massachusetts with Julia, his wife of twenty years, and three daughters, Chloë, Sadie and Elsa. He is a former academic who left university life for the challenges of the business world and is currently an Executive Vice President at a global consulting firm. His passions include an old farmhouse on Cape Cod, his workshop and tools, a 1940 Farmall tractor, and a 1949 Chevrolet pickup truck.

He earned his PhD and Master's from Oxford University, where he also taught, and his BA from Trinity College in Hartford, Connecticut. He earned his high school diploma from The Hill School in Pottstown, Pennsylvania.

His poems have appeared in a number of publications; and his articles, interviews and reviews have been published by *Poetry Review, The Times Literary Supplement, Times Higher Education Supplement, New Writing, Notes & Queries,* and *Oxford Today.*

This book is set in Garamond Premier Pro, which had its genesis in 1988 when type-designer Robert Slimbach visited the Plantin-Moretus Museum in Antwerp, Belgium, to study its collection of Claude Garamond's metal punches and typefaces. During the mid-fifteen hundreds, Garamond—a Parisian punch-cutter—produced a refined array of book types that combined an unprecedented degree of balance and elegance, for centuries standing as the pinnacle of beauty and practicality in type-founding. Slimbach has created an entirely new interpretation based on Garamond's designs and on comparable italics cut by Robert Granjon, Garamond's contemporary.

To order additional copies of this book
or other Antrim House titles, contact the publisher at

Antrim House
21 Goodrich Rd., Simsbury, CT 06070
860.217.0023, AntrimHouse@comcast.net
or the house website (www.AntrimHouseBooks.com).

•

On the house website
in addition to information on books
you will find sample poems, upcoming events,
and a "seminar room" featuring supplemental biography,
notes, images, poems, reviews, and
writing suggestions.

CPSIA information can be obtained at www.ICGtesting.com
Printed in the USA
BVOW080048070313

314895BV00002B/9/P